Leaving Home II

Coming of age in the Navy

Bud Hunton

Copyright © 2024 by Bud Hunton

ISBN: 978-1-77883-440-0 (Paperback)

All rights reserved. No part of this publication may be reproduced, distributed, or transmitted in any form or by any means, including photocopying, recording, or other electronic or mechanical methods, without the prior written permission of the publisher, except in the case brief quotations embodied in critical reviews and other noncommercial uses permitted by copyright law.

The views expressed in this book are solely those of the author and do not necessarily reflect the views of the publisher, and the publisher hereby disclaims any responsibility for them.

BookSide Press
877-741-8091
www.booksidepress.com
orders@booksidepress.com

Contents

Prologue vi
Part 1   The Adventure Begins—Leaving Home 1

From Boot Camp to Hospital Corps School 5
The Buddy System 8
Stateside Again 12
1959–1963 13
Becoming a Professional 16
The Fleet Marine Force 19
U.S. Naval Hospital, Philadelphia 23
On the Road Again—Leaving Philly 25
Aboard the USS Robert H. McCard *(DD-822)* 26
Getting Underway 27
Visiting England 28

Part 2   Coming Home (1975–2012) — Civilian Careers
              after Navy Retirement 32

Grandview Hospital—Department of Radiology 34
Time to Move On 35
Education as a Career 36
1975–2012: Home Life with Family and Friends 39
Visiting with Relatives 42

Historical Events 44
Photos 46
Naval Terminology 50

Leaving Home

Autobiography of Bud W. Hunton
HMC USN, Retired

PROLOGUE

1943–1955: The Early Years

Born at the Children's Hospital of Philadelphia in Pennsylvania, on August 13, 1938, I spent most of my early childhood in Philadelphia. Dad was a truck driver from the Philadelphia area and came from a large family consisting of twenty-two siblings. I only remember three of his sisters and two of his brothers. As a truck driver, he was frequently on the road, so memories of him at home were scarce.

My earliest memories go back to an area of Philadelphia known as Manayunk, located in lower Northwest Philly. It was in this area that my dad, Harry Pearson Hunton, met Bud Goodwin, and they became good friends, eventually giving Mom and Dad the idea of naming me Bud.

Mag and Bud Goodwin (circa 1950) near Route 33

Gertrude Hunton with her five children

Prior to 1955, my earliest memories go back to the age of five, when my family moved from Philadelphia, Pennsylvania, to a small farm two and a half miles west of Wapakoneta, Ohio. In the late thirties and early forties, my dad worked with his friend Bud Goodwin delivering coal in the Philadelphia area. This apparently was the start of my dad's truck-driving career and the beginning of a long

Leaving Home II

friendship between the two men.

In 1938, when I was born, Dad and Mom decided to name me Bud,[1] after Bud Goodwin, who then became my godfather. As I grew up, Bud started taking me back to Ohio with him in his dump truck. At about the age of five or six, I stayed with Bud's sister, Mary, when she lived in a part of St. Marys called Rabbit Town, a kind of low-rent area for the times. Mary and her husband, Ike Stoker, always made me feel welcome, and I shared a room with her two youngest kids, Linda and Buddy.

Bud and his wife, Mag, were Ohio natives and living on a small five-acre farm owned by Bud. The adjacent property was owned by his brother Frank "Doc" Goodwin. Frank's wife was Althea. She was a very friendly lady who apparently was a great mother. Her children—Shirley, Bruce, Sandy, and Margaret—were close to the Hunton kids, and we played well together and attended Moulton Elementary School in Moulton, Ohio.

On the farm, there was a large barn, two horses, several chickens, and a few pigs and goats. A white goat that we called Snowball was my favorite and became my pet. The house that we moved into was an old log house that eventually was redone with wood over the logs. There was no electric or running water. Our water source was a well that we pumped by hand. We used kerosene lamps at night. Our source of heat was a potbelly stove in the small living room, which also heated the upstairs via a vent in the ceiling. We used coal or wood, whatever was available at the time.

As kids, we all enjoyed the animals and learned a bit about farm life by helping with the chores. At one point, all five of us kids were attending Moulton. Unfortunately, when Pete was dealing with polio, he was quarantined to the house and missed school for several months. Eventually, Mrs. Gearing was able to homeschool Pete, and he did okay after that.

At the time of our move, around 1943, I was starting the third grade at Moulton Elementary School, approximately three miles away. We were picked up and dropped off by a school bus. I only remember a few of the Moulton kids, including Doris (Hemmelgarn) Makley. Doris was the future wife of Bob Makley, my future brother-in-law. All five of us kids packed our lunch and noticed that most of the other kids ate at the school cafeteria. It was a rare treat when Mom, Gertrude Hunton, was able to send money with us to buy our lunches. I finished the eighth grade at Moulton and ended up living with my mom while going to Blume High School in Wapakoneta.

My early teen years were unsupervised and left me feeling insecure. Like a lot of teenagers that age, I drifted into a small group of juveniles who were into stealing hubcaps and other minor issues. Once my Dad got wind of this, I was forced to move to Brazil, Indiana, and live with Dad and Tina. Brother Pete had already moved there and was working as a dispatcher for a local cab company. I have fond memories of me and Pete eating "TV bologna" and watching Steve Allen on late-night TV.

Brazil was a nice town, However, I missed family and friends from Ohio. Dad's wife, Tina, treated us well, and we all got along. When Dad started working for a different trucking company out of Akron, Ohio, I moved back to Wapak and stayed with my mom and brother Pete in Wapak, Ohio. Dad's last move before retiring was to Grove City, near Columbus, Ohio.

Tina was working for a Fotomat store in a parking lot when she passed away. It was a very unusual story. Apparently, Tina was leaving the Fotomat at the end of her shift and was attempting to pick up a large envelope that had fallen onto the roadway. Tina was short and obese, and when she opened her car door and reached down to retrieve the envelope, she lost her balance and then fell from the car. The car rolled over her body, killing her instantly.

Bev and I attended her funeral in Grove City. Dad was in a very good mood that day. During the viewing, Dad placed her bingo cards in the coffin with her. He seemed to be doing stand-up comedy during the viewing, moving from group to group, leaving then laughing or a least with a smile on their face. This was just Dad's way of dealing with death.

He showed me a pistol that he was carrying in his coat pocket and said, "This is just in case she tries to get up." Only people who knew of Dad and Tina's stormy relationship understood this.

Since I was only seventeen, my parents had to accompany me to the recruiting office along with my birth certificate and then sign for approval for me to enlist for what was known as a kitty cruise, defined as "an enlistment in the United States Navy starting before one's eighteenth birthday and therefore ending before one's twenty-first." I remember my mother crying and my dad telling her that this was going to be a great opportunity for me.

When we moved to Ohio, I was in the third grade and had only experienced city life. Bud Goodwin's Ohio family—brother Frank Goodwin, sister-in-law Althea, and three children—lived a short distance down the road, where I met Bruce Goodwin, eldest of Frank Goodwin's children. Bud's nephew, Bruce Goodwin, was a few years older than me and would turn out to be like a big brother. Over the next eleven years, Bruce and I fished, swam, and hunted small game together and eventually learned to roller-skate. Roller skating allowed us to meet young ladies at the skating rink. Bruce was my mentor through high school, and then he joined the marines and shipped out for basic training.

Another neighbor named Jerry McHaffey would often join us during our teenage escapades. Jerry joined the navy about a year or so before I did, and we eventually met a few years later in Yokosuka, Japan, where his ship pulled into Yokosuka for shore leave (also known as liberty). I ran into Jerry at a local bar, and we caught up on our navy travels over a couple of beers. That was the last time I would see Jerry alive.

Although I talked my parents into letting me drop out of the last year of high school, I would eventually earn three college degrees—master's, bachelor's, and associate's—from three different colleges. I accomplished this a few years before my mother passed away, making her very happy and proud. I would eventually marry and produce seventeen grandchildren and great- grandchildren.

After retiring from the navy in 1975, I worked at as a manager of radiology departments in Cincinnati and Dayton for a few years and ended up teaching at Sinclair Community College for the remainder of my working career. While I was working full-time at local hospitals and then college, there were good opportunities to work for book-publishing companies on line-editing medical textbooks and writing columns for magazines such as the *Advance in Radiology* magazine. I published dozens of columns pertaining to the field of radiology in the 1980s and edited medical textbooks for a publishing company in Chicago.

PART 1

THE ADVENTURE BEGINS—LEAVING HOME

> *By leaving behind your old self and taking a leap of faith into the unknown, you find out what you are truly capable of becoming.* — Unknown

At the age of seventeen, I began my journey with a bus trip to Fort Hayes in Columbus, Ohio, to get a physical examination. The day went by quickly, and then the inductees were loaded onto a train heading for Chicago, Illinois, and then on to the U.S. Naval Training Center at Great Lakes, Illinois. The training, known as "boot camp," lasted approximately eight weeks. It was located on the western shore of Lake Michigan, thirty-six miles north of Chicago.

This was the start of my twenty-year navy career that would take me through several duty stations in the United States and sea duty tours that would take me to far away from Wapakoneta, Ohio. "Join the navy and see the world," as the saying used to go. I did see my share of travel. After my training was completed at Great Lakes, Illinois, I eventually traveled to San Francisco, California, by train and then on to Yokosuka, Japan, courtesy of the U.S. Air Force.

I spent my preteen years in a small town named Wapakoneta, located in the southwestern part of Ohio. I did grade school at Moulton, Ohio, until the eighth grade and then went to Blume High in Wapakoneta, Ohio. While I was a teenager, summers were spent working on the farm where we lived or neighboring farms, making fifty cents an hour plus free lunch.

Wapakoneta is an Indian name. Wapak was the chief of the local Shawnee tribe, and Koneta was his wife. Some of the older folks from the area claim Indian heritage. Wapak, as it is commonly called, gained popularity in 1969 when a local man named Neil Armstrong landed on the moon. Wapak will celebrate the fiftieth anniversary of this event on July 20, 2019. Wapak was visited by several celebrities during this time, and it was noted by comedian Bob Hope that it was the only place in the United States where you could still make a phone call for five cents.

Pay phones in Wapakoneta, Ohio. | Calls could be made for five cents. | Moulton Elementary School.

Navy Boot Camp | Service school barracks, 1956.

In late August 1955, I arrived at the U.S. Naval Training Center at Great Lakes, Illinois. This was the beginning of my kitty cruise. As a young man, I had rarely traveled outside of Ohio. However, after joining the navy, I experienced fantastic travels to locations near the Great Lakes training center, such as Chicago and Milwaukee. On weekends after boot camp, I traveled to dance halls such as the Roof in Milwaukee or the Playboy Club in downtown Chicago. My

Leaving Home II

buddies from the base were older than me and would accompany me on these trips. We used what was referred to as the "buddy system," meaning that we were looking out for one another.

Arriving at the base early in the morning via bus from Union Station in Chicago, we were introduced to the "chow hall" and lined up for breakfast. We were all amazed at the activity around us, and we could smell food cooking at the chow hall. This was some of the best food I had ever experienced—fresh fruit of all kinds, fried or scrambled eggs, biscuits and gravy, and a host of items I had never seen before.

After breakfast, we were quickly assigned to a barracks and a company number and then introduced to our company commander. The eight weeks at boot camp went by quickly and seem to instill in us the motivation to survive at sea and understand why discipline was important. Feeling "salty," as they used to say, we were ready for graduation. My mother and father were both there, accompanied by Tina along with elder sister Margaret and her husband, Marion.

My company commander was a newly promoted chief by the name of McGinty who had seen action in the Pacific during World War II. By comparison to other company commanders, he seemed like a very nice guy. On an occasional day that McGinty could not be with us, a substitute commander such as Choker Thomas would be our instructor. His name said it all. When we had to fall out on the "grinder" at 0400, no one complained out loud. Choker Thomas was an African American sailor with a reputation of being the meanest company commander at Great Lakes.

The weeks in boot camp went by quickly, leaving memories of early-morning PT and great food in the chow hall. Aside from shoveling snow to clear the streets, everything else was fairly easy. While stationed at Great Lakes Naval Hospital, I was able to travel home on weekends either to Lima, Ohio, just twelve miles from my hometown of Wapakoneta (Wapak), or to Brazil, Indiana, to visit Dad and stepmom Tina. The round-trip train fare was approximately $8.50, and I could be home in a few hours.

Although I was only seventeen years old when I had started my weekend train travels, I would usually sit in what was known as the bar car or club car and drink beer on the way home. I quickly learned that although I was under the legal drinking age of eighteen for beer and twenty-one for whiskey, being in uniform granted me certain privileges. In those days, beer that was 3.2 percent alcohol was usually reserved for the younger drinkers and was also sold as draft beer in gallon jugs. I learned to drink in moderation, fearing being scolded by my elder sister or dad. I continued drinking in moderation, not for fear of scolding, just learning to keep a clear head for any medical emergencies, which I will discuss later.

Boot camp went by quickly, as did females in the bar car of the train. During the trips from Chicago to Lima, I was often able to meet pretty young ladies (usually in their mid-twenties to early thirties). Unfortunately, I had always arranged for someone to meet me at the train station in Lima, usually my elder sister Margaret (Aggie). Aggie and her husband, Marion, would pick me up at the train station in Lima, Ohio, and we would stop at one of Marion's favorite bars on the way home for a tenderloin sandwich and a few beers. Looking back on those days, I imagine how different life may have been if cell phones were invented earlier.

Leaving Home II

Charleston group

From Boot Camp to Hospital Corps School

After graduation from boot camp, I was assigned to Hospital Corps School, also located at the naval base at Great Lakes, Illinois. The hospital compound consisted of wood-frame buildings similar to the naval training center. This was a post–World War II construction era, and eventually, a hospital would be built using bricks and mortar. Years later, I would return to this area to see my nephew Kevin Jackson graduate from boot camp and then Hospital Corps School months later. Corps School was basic medical training, including basic medical terminology, anatomy and physiology, pharmacology, and first aid.

Up until the late forties and the end of World War II, hospital corpsmen were known as pharmacist mates. Most corpsmen were assigned directly to a land-based hospital or ship after completion of the program. It was my fortune to be assigned to the U.S. Naval Hospital at Great Lakes, Illinois. Our training was in the 1955-era corps school, also known as "A-school." I met my first friend, Rick Daffron, during corps school. We teamed up with two air force students, and the four of us bought an old car to get around in. Corpsmen were permitted to leave the base every other night and every other weekend. We had some great times with the old car.

My first hospital assignment was to Ward 74 South, a neurosurgical ward. The patients who were admitted here were active-duty service members from various branches of the service who had been diagnosed with neurological traumas or disorders. I can only remember one patient whom I had encountered while I was assigned there. His name was Michael. He was in the army and home on leave when he and a few friends decided to take a swim in Lake Michigan. Apparently, Michael dove into the water, striking his head, causing injury to his cervical spine (neck). The ensuing injury caused paralysis.

Memorial

Leaving Home II

When I had encountered him, Michael was on a device known as a Stryker frame, equipment designed for patients who were paralyzed. In Michael's case, he was paralyzed from the neck down. As a ward corpsman, I was trained to turn Michael over every few hours. This would help avoid decubitus ulcers or bedsores, as they were commonly known. Bedsores can become infected and cause complications, so it was important to ensure that we maintained a schedule. We worked in teams of two to safely turn Michael over, face up to face down or vice versa.

I have to add that patients become depressed after a few weeks of this routine and often have to seek a psychiatric consultation. After six months of duty on Ward 74 South, I was transferred to a new assignment at the hospital's special services department. I now helped organized special events and maintained athletic equipment. The weekend always went by quickly, and by Sunday evening, I was on the train from Lima to Chicago, heading back to the Great Lakes naval base. After arriving at Union Station on the south side of Chicago, I headed for the North Shore Line, an elevated train that would take me directly to the naval base and hospital.

Union Station, Chicago, 1950s.   South State Street, Chicago, 1950s.

The Buddy System

I usually arrived in Chicago late at night and caught the North Shore Line to the naval base. There were always several other sailors heading back at this time of the evening, and I can remember how we used the buddy system for safety and stayed together while navigating northward on State Street on the way to the North Shore Line. There was always a group of homeless guys along the sidewalk looking for handouts. My first incident with this group scared me. They intentionally blocked the sidewalk while they approached us like a bunch of zombies from *The Walking Dead* with their hands out.

An old salt who was in uniform like the rest of us said, "Watch this."

He then threw a handful of coins, mostly pennies and nickels, into the middle of State Street. The sound of coins hitting the street quickly caught their attention, and they scrambled out into traffic to recover the coins. I can still remember the sound of horns and brakes when they rushed into the street. Fortunately, I do not recall anyone ever getting injured during these incidents.

I received a clear understanding of the buddy system that kept me safe on the nights I returned from liberty and navigated the streets of Chicago. As I grew older and traveled the world, the buddy system became part of my personality in foreign ports or any area where I did not have a good comfort level. In foreign countries, we would always leave the ship in small groups of four or five. When in unfamiliar bars or restaurants, we always sat facing the door and used hand signals to indicate that something was suspicious.

Leaving Home II

North Shore Line, Chicago, Illinois.

While stationed at Great Lakes, I would occasionally have a night out in Milwaukee, just north of the base, and there was an USO that I would go to with a few buddies. Our favorite weekend hangout was a dance hall known as the Roof—good dance music and a lot of young ladies. Rick Daffron and I spent a lot of time together during our "liberty" or off-duty hours. On my weekends off, I would also head back home via Lima, Ohio, to visit family and friends in the Wapak/St. Marys area of Ohio. On alternate weekends, I would also visit a beautiful young lady named Angie Nichols, a girl I had met while visiting Dad and Tina when they lived in Brazil, Indiana.

My tour of duty at Great Lakes, Illinois, ended in the summer of 1957. I was nineteen years old and halfway through my four-year enlistment. I had received orders to the U.S. Naval Hospital in Yokosuka, Japan, a place that neither I nor anyone I knew had ever heard of. To prepare for this journey, I went to the hospital library and did some research on the country. In addition, I checked out a couple of audio tapes to assist me in learning some basic Japanese language. After saying farewell to family and friends, I then traveled by train from Lima, Ohio, to San Francisco, California.

Undoubtedly, this was the most exciting event I had experienced in my lifetime. The views from the train window were beautiful and changed each day. Upon arriving in San Francisco, I was assigned to a holding company on the naval base. The sailors here were all waiting for transportation to their next duty station, and everyone was assigned some type of daily task such as kitchen duty or cleaning the barracks while we waited for our orders to transfer out.

About ten days after my arrival, I boarded a military flight from Travis Air Force Base headed for Tokyo, Japan. It was a no-frills flight and very uncomfortable. It was a large plane filled with various military people headed for Japan. We sat in some type of cargo netting instead of regular seats.

From Travis, we headed west over the Pacific to Hawaii and landed at Hickam Air Force Base to refuel and get something to eat. We continued on to our next stop, Wake Island, where we refueled before completing our flight to Japan. After we had arrived in Tokyo, there were several military buses waiting to take us to our appropriate duty stations. Army, marines, and navy were among this tired group. After several hours of airtime, we all felt a sense of relief knowing that we were finally on the last leg of our journey. After checking into the corpsman's barracks at the naval hospital in Yokosuka, I finally slept in one of the most comfortable bunk beds I had ever slept in. It seemed like I had not slept in several days.

I loved the duty in Japan. In addition to movies and bowling alleys, the naval base offered recreation such as sailing and fishing and endless opportunities to travel to various cities throughout Japan. The base special services department also offered lodging at unique places in the mountains. Trout fishing near the hotel was great, and the hotel would cook whatever you caught and serve it for your dinner that evening.

The only trauma I had observed while stationed at Yokosuka was the crash of a military helicopter, killing all on board. As part of the investigation, I was assigned to the X-ray department to assist with the autopsy. We carefully placed each of the remains on the X-ray table to take X-rays that would look for any possible foul play that may have occurred.

My corpsmen buddies, HN John Campbell and HM3 Steve Ferris, traveled with me on a few trips. The three of us also took up sailing and would check out a sailboat for the weekend and sail around the bay area. Once, while swimming from our sailboat to the beach, Steve and I became exhausted and almost drowned. Fortunately, two Japanese fishermen came to our rescue and took us ashore. We also made a few trips to Tokyo to shop at Ginza, a well-known Japanese shopping district, to buy some great souvenirs. The three of us also spent a weekend climbing part of Mount Fuji.

U.S. Naval Hospital, Yokosuka, Japan, 1957.

Mount Fuji, Japan.

In July 1959, I was transferred from the naval hospital in Yokosuka to the USS *Dixie* (AD-14). She was providing service to the Seventh

Fleet at the time and was due to return to the United States.

While aboard the *Dixie*, I was assigned to sick bay along with three other corpsmen who were being transferred to the States for discharge. Our time working in the *Dixie*'s sick bay was interesting, to say the least. I had never been aboard a ship before, so seeing how this part of the navy worked was very interesting and gave us transient corpsmen an insight to what sea duty could be. We were headed for San Diego, California, to receive our discharge papers from the navy and be on our way to civilian life.

We only made one stop on our way back home. However, it was one of the most memorable weeks in my life. The ship tied up at the naval base in Hawaii for refueling and replenishment. We were only there for about a week, and the time flew by. As transients, the other three corpsmen and I were permitted unlimited liberty to explore the island. The four of us rented a car and took off for parts unknown. The beach was fantastic, and the water was great. We swam and surfed as best we could.

One of the corpsmen (I can't recall his name) stated that he was going to check with the ship's personnel department to see if he could be discharged here instead of California. When we got underway, he was nowhere to be seen, so I am assuming that he stayed in Hawaii. While we were touring the beach in our rental car, he often commented that he would like to stay in Hawaii and start a little business on the beach, such as renting surfboards, umbrellas, and such. That was fifty-eight years ago. He is probably a retired millionaire by now.

Stateside Again

The *Dixie*'s next stop was at the U.S. Naval Base in San Diego, California, in early August 1959. My discharge was due before my twenty-first birthday in August. I was assigned to the barracks at the naval base until my transportation was arranged via train back to Lima, Ohio. It was an interesting and long train ride from San Diego, California, to Lima, Ohio. That would be the last interstate train ride that I would ever take, so I soaked up the scenery and enjoyed the ride.

Once I had settled in back home on August 1959, I lived with my brother Pete and our mother in Wapak. I spent the next two months looking for work, interviewed for a few jobs, and settled for being a salesman with the Omar Bread Company, located in Sidney, Ohio, about twenty miles south of Wapak.

They sent me to Columbus, Ohio, for a weeklong course on basic salesmanship. Afterward, I was assigned to the Omar plant in Sidney. The pay for this job was $137 per week plus a commission on what you sold from the truck, actually a decent salary for those days. My career with Omar ended after I had an unpleasant encounter with a supervisor who showed up on my route and admonished me for not having my tie on properly. It kind of reminded me of my navy days when you were told how to wear your hat. I was at the recruiter's office shortly after that.

1959–1963

When I spoke to the navy recruiters, I was offered a reenlistment bonus (approximately $3,000) plus my choice of service schools. I had already been giving this some thought and had decided on X-ray school. My father had suggested this to me on a few occasions.

I started dating Beverly shortly after my discharge from the navy in August. It was now mid-October 1959, and I had decided to reenlist in the navy and asked Bev to marry me. This did not sit well with her family, particularly her father, John. After much discussion with Bev, we eloped to Redkey, Indiana, where we were married on October 24, 1959. Aggie and Marion went with us. Bev and I stayed in a small apartment owned by my sister Sally in Wapakoneta, Ohio. Sally informed me that Bev's three elder brothers were out looking for me, seeking revenge for taking their sister away from home. Bev was eighteen years old at the time.

I was then sent to the U.S. Naval Receiving Station in Washington, D.C., to wait for orders to X-ray school. My sister and her husband drove Bev and I to the Greyhound station in Lima, Ohio, to get a ride to Washington, D.C. Unfortunately, I forgot to give Bev my car keys, so I had to mail then to her from DC. She was staying at my sister's house at the time, so she was able to get a ride back home with her.

Once I received my orders and returned home, we packed everything that we had in a 1959 Ford convertible and headed for Philadelphia, stopping in Akron, Ohio, to visit with my dad and Tina. Tina was very happy that we were married and baked us a wedding cake. We then headed for my new duty station at the U.S. Naval Hospital in Philadelphia, Pennsylvania.

We stopped for a short visit at my aunt Eleanor's house in North Philly. It was in an area of what was referred to as row homes. The homes were all connected and consisted of a living room and kitchen on the first floor and two or three bedrooms on the second floor. All homes had a full basement plus a door leading to a fenced-in backyard. As far as I know, this was the only place they had ever lived. My other aunt Mildred and her husband, George, lived a few blocks away in a similar row home.

Eleanor and husband Fred were very helpful, giving us advice on how to get to the hospital from their house. They were very hospitable and invited us back for Sunday dinners over the years. Uncle Fred delivered beer in the North Philadelphia area. He was a very comical character and would usually answer the door with a beer in his hand. His directions to the naval hospital were spot on. Turns out it was a straight drive down Broad Street, which ends at the naval base.

We rented a furnished apartment just off Broad at McKean Street for $60 a month. Our apartment consisted of a small kitchen and bedroom plus a shared bathroom and shower. The folks whom we had rented from were older Italian immigrants, some of the kindest people we had ever met.

The naval hospital was a short fifteen-minute drive from our apartment. The hospital was located on South Broad Street, directly across from Veterans Stadium. During my three tours of duty, I would enjoy several sporting events at the stadium, including the army-versus-navy football games. During our first year in Philadelphia, I took Bev to the Mummers Parade on New Year's Day. The parade was always held on Broad Street, so it was easy to find. We had a great time, and I still recall explaining to Bev that all the folks in the parade were men.

There were only five students in our class of radiology students. Although our class did not officially start until January 1, 1960, we were immediately put to work in the X-ray department, working under the supervision of a registered radiologic technologist. The U.S. Navy's X-ray program was officially listed as a twelve-month program, although most attendees put in a few additional months of training, waiting for the program to officially begin.

Going to Philadelphia for X-ray school would be the first of our moving and traveling adventures. We still have fond memories of all three of our tours of duty there. The U.S. Naval Hospital was a twelve-story structure that covered a few city blocks. There were wooden structures that were attached at ground-floor level and ran from the main hospital to various side streets in South Philadelphia. During later years as a chief petty officer, I would patrol the ramps on a motorized scooter, covering several city blocks of riding for security purposes during the Vietnam era, when the hospital was receiving bomb threats.

Becoming a Professional

I graduated from X-ray school in 1960 and continued to work on as a staff technologist. In 1961, I sat for the national radiologic technologist examination. My four classmates and I showed up at the exam center, located in a large inner city hospital. We were wearing our dress blues, and until that day, we did not realize that the radiology profession (X-ray) was composed of a majority of females. I can still remember the five of us walking into the exam room in our dress blue uniforms. We were surrounded by a sea of white uniforms as the exam proctor motioned for us to have a seat. Judging by the looks on their faces, the others sitting for the test were as surprised as we were. We were plagued with questions by pretty young ladies as soon as the test was over.

Upon completion of the radiology program in Philadelphia, I stayed on as a staff radiographer, continuing to take X-rays on a daily basis. The program was very successful and was staffed by a navy chief corpsman teaching positioning techniques, a radiologist (MD) teaching anatomy, and a medical physicist teaching physics.

Male radiographers were in short supply at this time, and here were several opportunities to work part-time as a radiographer (X-ray tech). One of my first civilian part-time jobs was at the Methodist hospital on Broad Street, ten minutes away from our apartment. My

Leaving Home II

basic function was to provide emergency X-ray services. It was a difficult job and kept me busy at all hours of the night. This was my first experience working with cases such as automobile accidents involving serious trauma and injuries.

In 1963, I received new orders for the U.S. Naval Hospital in Portsmouth, Virginia, for the purpose of training. I was headed for B-school, otherwise known as independent duty school. In Portsmouth, corpsmen were trained to serve on ships that did not have a doctor on board. B-school was a precursor for what is currently known as a physician's assistant. Our six months of training consisted of pharmacology (the study of various drugs), anatomy and physiology, and first aid and minor surgery. We packed up and headed South with our two daughters—Patty, born in 1960, and Susan, born in 1963.

Good friends were made while at Portsmouth, including John Stahler, who was also a radiologic technologist. We both had achieved the rank of HM2 (E-5) and would meet again when I returned to Philly in 1967.

After completing B-school, I was transferred to Norfolk, Virginia, where I was now assigned to my first ship, the USS *Rankin* (AKA-103), home-ported in Norfolk, Virginia. The *Rankin* was my first real sea duty, although it was not an independent duty assignment. There were five other corpsmen aboard plus a medical officer. The *Rankin* was classified as a Tolland-class attack cargo ship that was built during World War II. We had a large sick bay with beds for patients and a treatment room with X-ray and lab equipment.

Our missions usually included transporting troops and equipment to designated areas for the completion of their missions. On some deployments, we carried a U.S. Navy SEAL team. The SEAL team would use the deployment to practice their skills. They always had one hospital corpsman with their group who would usually come by the sick bay to replenish their medical supplies. The corpsmen of the *Rankin* whom I remember are HM2 Roger Labonte, HN Wayne Forbes, HN Tom Strayer, HM3 Burgess, and HM3 Gibbs.

I only ran into one of the *Rankin* corpsmen after leaving the ship—Wayne Forbes, who was a patient at the naval hospital in Philly when I did my next tour of duty there in 1967. Although I had looked forward to actually going on independent duty, having other corpsmen aboard was a good experience with a great sense of camaraderie. After a few short months aboard, we deployed for Guantanamo Bay, Cuba (Gitmo), for a period of refresher training, also known as operational readiness inspection (ORI).

My only memories of Gitmo are ridding the LCM to the pier to attend the evening shows at the enlisted men's club and then riding in the cattle cars from the club to the pier. "Cattle cars" is how the enlisted men referred to the crude trailers used to transport men to the pier, where a smaller boat would take them to their ship anchored in the bay. They were always crowded and did not offer any seats or means of support. Needless to say, someone always ended up on the floor.

From Gitmo, we continued to cruise into the Caribbean, where, during a squadron exercise in April 1965, *Rankin* participated in the Dominican Republic Intervention. Shortly arriving off the coast of Santa Domingo, our crew began the mass evacuation of civilians. We commenced the mass embarkation and evacuation of over one thousand refugees and U.S. nationals. I had always wondered why we had baby diapers, powdered milk, sanitary napkins, and other unusual items in our supply locker, and now I knew. Medical corpsmen were required to ride the LCM into the pier to assist with evacuating civilians. The bosun's mate, driving the LCM toward the pickup point, was carrying a .45-caliber pistol. Plus, his assistant had a machine gun just in case we encountered any problems with the insurgents.

There was an occasional *ping* against the steel wall as we went up the waterway toward the pier. However, we were well protected by the LCM's heavy armor. As a result of this operation, the *Rankin* and all her personnel were awarded the navy unit commendation by the secretary of the navy. I reenlisted aboard the *Rankin* in 1965 and, shortly afterward, received orders to the Second Marine Division at Camp Lejune, North Carolina.

The Fleet Marine Force

My assignment there was to the First Battalion, Eighth Marine Regiment, affectionately known as the "grunts." At Camp Lejune, groups of hospital corpsmen were issued marine corps uniforms with navy-rating badges and then trained for a couple of months for field medicine or how to handle casualties during combat conditions. Most of our medical instructors were corpsmen who had served in Korea or Vietnam or both.

Bud Hunton

HM2 Hunton at Camp Lejune, North Carolina.

LCM used to transport troops or crew.

Leaving Home II

Our instructors for the military part of our education were excellent examples of marines. We did the usual hiking with full backpacks plus the physical training that went along with working with marines. In short, my first two months at Camp Lejune were spent learning how to function as a corpsman under combat conditions. Our instructors were all veterans of Vietnam, and the training we received was meant to save our lives and the lives of those we were helping. Our training program was part of the FMF (fleet marine force) experience. We now had to blend in and function under combat circumstances.

We wore marine corps uniforms with navy-rating badges to identify who the guys marching out of step were. Whenever we went on bivouac, the marines version of camping, my only fears were about snakes. The woods around Camp Lejune were notorious for the variety of snakes that lived there. Snake bites were a common occurrence, and the base dispensary was always reminding everyone to be careful when jumping into trenches.

At one point, the dispensary attempted to help the situation by sending out a memo informing all marines and navy corpsmen to bring in the particular snake that had bitten someone to help identify what specific type of snake was involved. A few days later, a few marines brought in a pizza box with a snake inside. When the dispensary corpsman opened the box, a rattlesnake slide out onto the floor, creating a small panic. The culprit was captured and expedited. A new memo went out the next day, adding two important words: "Dead Snake."

Shortly after training, our battalion was deployed on a Med cruise aboard the USS *Sandoval* (APA-194). The crew quarters were packed and dimly lit. The arrangement of bunks stacked five high was a sight that I disliked, having had more comfortable bedding arrangements aboard the *Rankin*. Unfortunately, whenever a drunk marine was carried back to the ship, for safety reasons, the intoxicated person was hoisted by rope to his appropriate bunk. It was comical to see a bunch of drunk marines hoisting someone up to their rack (bunk). Needless to say, I was quite pleased to learn that I had passed the exam for HM1 E-6 and was transferred to the staff NCO quarters.

HM1/E-6 was the marine equivalent of a staff NCO. The NCO quarters had much nicer accommodations, including thicker bunks stacked only two high. Their quarters were well lit and much closer to the main deck, and E-6– enlisted men were given separate dining areas as well as quarters. Our cruise was cut short, and the war ship headed back to Moorehead City, North Carolina, where we disembarked and returned to Camp Lejune. A few days after our return, we were informed that the First Battalion, Eighth Marines, would be deployed to Vietnam.

HMC Chester Bullard was our H Company chief. He approached me one morning at the staging area, where we were boxing up files and medical supplies, and told me to unpack my gear and report to headquarters to pick up my orders for the U.S. Naval Hospital in Philadelphia, Pennsylvania. I had mixed emotions. I was delighted not to be headed into a combat zone. However, I had become good friends with several of the corpsmen and felt bad for them. I could see them talking to the chief as I was leaving, asking him questions such as "Why doesn't Hunton have to go?"

As I drove away from our company area, I noticed that a group of corpsmen had gathered around the chief. I felt relieved that I did not have to leave Bev and the girls for a tour of duty in Vietnam. When I spoke to the chief earlier, he had informed me that my prior tour of duty aboard the USS *Rankin* (AKA- 103) plus my time at Camp Lejune had fulfilled my sea duty requirements, and I was now due to rotate back to shore duty. I said my goodbyes to all the corpsmen who were present and went by headquarters to pick up my new

Leaving Home II

orders. As I left the area, waving at the guys, I knew that I would never see some of them again. At home, it was great to give Bev the good news. She was ecstatic, and we were both very grateful.

This incident was in my memory for quite a while. My questions regarding what had happened once they arrived in Vietnam were partially answered when we visited the memorial in Washington, D.C. I was able to find at least three names of the corpsmen I remembered. After taking leave to be with family in Ohio, I reported for my second tour of duty at the naval hospital in Philly. We had four daughters now, and we found the location and quality of the new government housing to be very nice. It was conveniently located down the street from the hospital.

U.S. Naval Hospital, Philadelphia

I checked in at the hospital and was assigned to the radiology department, still located on the third floor. As the supervising petty officer, one of my primary duties was to keep the work flowing and ensure our tasks were being completed on time.

About three weeks into the job, I was making routine rounds to ensure everything was moving along smoothly. I heard my name being called from the area where the carts were located near our regular waiting area. As I approached the carts, I recognized a corpsman lying on a cart who apparently had been injured. He, along with a couple of other corpsmen, had just been brought in by air evac.

The H Company from Camp Lejune had apparently been attacked and fragged by explosive satchels shortly after arrival in Vietnam. Most of these brave young men had lost at least one leg and an arm on the same side of their body. One of the men informed me how lucky he felt to have impregnated his wife shortly before leaving for Vietnam. It seemed that he had also lost his testicles during the attack. He rattled off a list of casualties, and I truly felt sad for them, and at the same time, I was thinking how fortunate I was to have had the eighteen months of sea duty accrued when I was transferred to Camp Lejune, North Carolina.

During the day, my time was occupied in the radiology department, taking X-rays and supervising fifteen to twenty corpsmen who had been trained for radiology. After 4:00 p.m. or 1600, I was assigned to group two security. It was my job to patrol the hospital, especially the surrounding structures, known as wards. In the sixties, the naval hospital in Philly was the amputee center for the East Coast. Hundreds of amputees were evacuated from the West Coast to Philly for the much-needed orthopedic services. The radiology department was now strategically located on the third floor along with surgery. My hospital security rounds were made on a motorized scooter, and I always had at least two or three "deputies" riding along with me to deal with fights that often erupted in the amputee wards.

Leaving Home II

Old Salts

On the Road Again—Leaving Philly

In 1968, I received orders to the USS *Robert H. McCard* (DD-822), home-ported in Charleston, South Carolina. We rented a very nice house in Goose Creek, just a few miles north of the naval base. Within a year, we were assigned government quarters in Mendel Rivers Park. The housing consisted of newer brick homes with nice amenities such as air conditioning and an enclosed patio. The only downside was the occasional black snake or water moccasin that ventured onto the property. We were never bitten. However, Bev was surprised when she had opened our kitchen cabinet and found a cottonmouth water moccasin wrapped around a wineglass, staring at her. We called base pest control, and they responded quickly and removed the intruder.

The *McCard* had just returned from the Western Pacific, where they had completed a mission off the coast of Vietnam. The *McCard* was a very busy destroyer, often referred to as a "fast-moving greyhound." After reporting aboard in late August 1969, I began preparing for a Med cruise that was scheduled.

Huntons at Charleston Naval Base

Aboard the USS Robert H. McCard *(DD-822)*

Our deployment was set for departure from Charleston Naval Base in October 1969 to return in January 1970. The crew consisted of several young sailors who had never been to sea, and they were excited to get underway to visit several foreign ports. This would be my fifth cruise. My first cruise was aboard the USS *Dixie* (AD-14) from Japan to Hawaii and then to San Diego for discharge. My second and third cruises were a Med cruise and a Caribbean cruise aboard the USS *Rankin* (AKA-103). The fourth cruise (Med cruise) was aboard the USS *Sandoval* with the marines. My fifth and sixth cruises were aboard the *McCard* (DD-822).

Getting Underway

I started making the usual preparations for getting underway—restocking supplies, updating medical records, and making medical consultations for any of the crew who needed referrals. It was an uneventful cruise, with the exception of a serious injury that occurred aboard when a cook had his jaw broken during a fight on the mess deck. He was transferred to a British hospital in Malta for surgery.

My four daughters were growing and were starting to ask questions about our frequent travel. Patty was ten, Sue seven, Linda six, and Debbie five. I explained that it was part of navy life and that we only had to move a couple more times before retiring from the navy. They were all good kids, then and now. We were now at a point where we still had unpacked boxes from our last move when I received orders to a new destination. Unfortunately, frequent school changes were difficult for the girls.

Charleston offered an excellent climate for recreation such as golf. I played several months each year and improved my golf score. In October 1971, we departed for what was to become my last Med cruise. While underway in the North Atlantic, the *McCard* struck an iceberg, creating a crack in the ship's hull. We were apparently taking on water and had to head for Northampton, England, to repair the ship's hull. This incident occurred during a NATO (North Atlantic Treaty Organization) operation.

Bud Hunton

Visiting England

We were forced to break away from the operation and head for dry dock in Northampton. We returned home in January 1971. It took about one week for repairs, and then we headed back to Charleston. Everyone enjoyed England, and fond memories were made of the occasion. During the day, we visited the local pub and enjoyed eating fish and chips. We returned home to Charleston in January 1971.

Shortly after returning to our home port in Charleston, I received my third set of orders for the U.S. Naval Hospital in Philadelphia, Pennsylvania. No more apartments or public housing this time. I was determined to provide a better quality of life for my family. With an increase in pay as a chief petty officer plus working as an X-ray technologist at a civilian hospital, I rented a very nice two-story house in Marlton, New Jersey. It was a twenty-five-minute drive across the Walt Whitman Bridge to New Jersey. We lived in a nice neighborhood with a fenced-in yard. The two-story home was very comfortable, and the local schools were somewhat better than we had seen in our travels.

In Philadelphia, I was now the department chief, which included a school of radiography plus a staff of twenty radiologic technologists (formerly known as X-ray technologists). We were a full-service imaging department and provided service to active duty and retired military as well as veterans. Unfortunately, antiwar factions were now calling in bomb threats to the hospital on a regular basis. When I stood duty after hours, my chief concern was for the safety and security of the hospital. I worked with the FBI on any active threats that were made on my watch or threats that were in existence when I assumed duty as chief of the day.

Leaving Home II

The hospital had now become the amputee center for the East Coast, and we housed hundreds of amputees who had recently returned from Vietnam. The hospital's third floor now consisted of orthopedics, the main operation room, and Radiology. As I was getting close to retirement, I reflected on the three tours of duty that I had completed, friends I had made, and the skills and education I had accrued.

The Philadelphia naval hospital was the first high-rise hospital building constructed by the U.S. Navy. It opened in 1935 with 650 beds and a total floor space of 352,000 square feet. The hospital was situated on forty-nine acres in the southern part of Philadelphia, bordered by Broad Street on the east and Pattison Avenue on the south. From the upper levels of the hospital, we had a good view of Veterans Stadium, located just across Broad Street. In addition to having perks such as free admission to football games, some of my fellow corpsmen did ride along with the ambulance to the annual Army–Navy Games. The hospital was demolished on June 9, 2001, at 7:02 a.m.

Statue of Sailor

Countries that I visited:

Japan
England
Monaco, France
Greece
Turkey
Italy
Spain
Virgin Islands (St. Croix, St. Thomas, Frederiksted)
Puerto Rico
Cuba
North Africa (Tunisia, Morocco)

Cruises:

Atlantic
North Atlantic (Blue Nose), crossed the Arctic Circle
Mediterranean
Caribbean

Part 2

Coming Home (1975–2012) — Civilian Careers after Navy Retirement

You can't go home again because home has ceased to exist except in the mothballs of memory. —John Steinbeck, *Travels with Charley*

My first civilian job was technical director of radiology at the St. Francis Hospital in Cincinnati, Ohio.[2] The hospital administrator flew me out for an interview and provided lodging at the hospital. My room was located at the hospital in what was described to me as the "nuns quarters." No room service, no phones, just a basic room with a bed and a bathroom. This should have been a clue to me that the hospital was having some budget problems. I confirmed this when I hired on and later discovered that my salary was low compared to other area hospitals.

The job only lasted for about ten months. I was then informed that St. Francis Hospital would be closing in a few months and merging with St. George Hospital in Cincinnati. Not sure if I would have a position at that time, I accepted a position as director of radiology for Grandview Hospital in Dayton, Ohio. Dayton is about an hour drive north to Wapak and St. Marys (Bev's home). Grandview was an osteopathic hospital, with a great medical staff and employees. Everyone I knew was very friendly, and I still receive Christmas cards from some of the staff.

During my interview, I noticed that the department had a lot of old X-ray equipment that was in need of updating, and apparently, the budgetary restrictions prevented much equipment replacement. Soon after assuming my new position, I began to bargain with various equipment companies to lease new imaging equipment. Within the next eighteen months, 80 percent of the department's equipment had been replaced, and we were well under budget. My performance ratings were high, and I was now earning annual bonuses.

Bud Hunton, retired at age thirty-seven.

Grandview was not my first osteopathic hospital. I had previously worked as a part-time X-ray tech, taking call at the Metropolitan Hospital in Philadelphia. My day job was at the naval hospital. At the Metropolitan Hospital, I worked ten days a month from 7:00 p.m. until 7:00 a.m. My patients all came through the hospital's emergency room, which was located directly across the street from Philadelphia's main police station. I was the first part-time RT employed by the hospital to cover the night shift. Previously, a full-time person covered radiology every night from 7:00 p.m. until 7:00 a.m. The department saved money by not having to pay benefits. Plus, they gained more expertise for trauma X-rays than they previously had. I had talked two other navy RTs into splitting the work with me, and we all agreed to work ten nights a month to cover the department after hours.

Bud Hunton

<u>Grandview Hospital—Department of Radiology</u>

Dr. Martin Landis was the chief radiologist who had interviewed and hired me for the position of administrative director of radiology at Grandview Hospital. He and five other radiologists had a contract with the hospital that included the right to have input on who was hired for the position.

My first five or so years at Grandview were very productive. After replacing the older equipment and adding new technology such as ultrasound, I had a proven track record of positive changes. By 1980, we had sixty-four full-time employees and five part-timers. The additional equipment had improved Grandview's imaging services and increased the revenue. I was now managing a multimillion-dollar department, and my achievements did not go unnoticed. I was asked to speak at local and state educational meetings and eventually wrote over fifty articles for technical magazines such as *Advance in Radiology*.

My previous experiences had shown that leasing was an economical way to replace older equipment. It enabled the hospital to update more equipment and services while spreading the cost via leasing. This change made the department radiologist very happy and, with budget cuts soon to appear, also put a smile on the face of the hospital administrator. A few short years after starting my job with Grandview, hospital administration decided to open an ambulatory care center approximately ten miles south of Dayton. I was given the responsibility for planning and staffing the new radiology department. At first, the new facility was called an ambulatory care center, and finally, when about fifty beds were added, it was then called Southview Hospital.

Grandview's radiology department was unique in that the cardiac cath lab was located within the department of radiology. In most hospitals, the cath lab is operated separately. This caused a bit of friction since the cardiologist technically was under the purview of the radiologist. I hired all personnel for the lab, and they reported directly to me.

In the early seventies, the cardiologist did several pacemaker implants, including some that were nuclear. Nuclear pacemakers were very expensive. Prices started at around $5,000 and went much higher. A basic pacemaker went for around $1,000 and often had to be replaced or adjusted in a few years. Recent articles had indicated that nuclear pacemakers have lasted as much as thirty-four years and continued to operate well. Grandview's cardiologist started using nuclear pacemakers shortly after I had started working there.

One of the downsides of the nuclear pacemakers was the fact that they contained plutonium. Plutonium is a radioactive element with the symbol Pu and atomic number 94. It was my job as administrative director to document all patients receiving a nuclear pacemaker. This could be a problem when patients could not be contacted as a matter of follow-up. It was then my job to notify the FBI, who would then follow up on the patient and try to make contact. It was discovered early on that some people were in cemeteries using special instruments to locate the pacemakers, dig them up, and resell them. Keep in mind that the plutonium in the pacemaker could also be used to make nuclear weapons.

Time to Move On

Being director of radiology for Grandview and Southview was a good position and a great learning experience for about ten years, at which time the hospital was sold to a much larger hospital and I was let go along with several others in middle management. When other hospital corporations are in the market to buy a smaller hospital, the first move of the smaller hospital is usually to reduce salary expenses to make the sale appear economically more attractive. I interviewed at out-of-town hospitals and considered a hospital south of Columbus, Ohio, in Chillicothe. However, I was approached by Sinclair Community College for a teaching position, which I accepted and maintained for twenty-two years.

Education as a Career

My last career change came when I was recruited by Sinclair Community College, a position that I held for twenty-two years before retiring. Within two weeks after leaving Grandview, I was contacted by Sinclair College and set up an interview. I started immediately, teaching radiology topics and doing clinicals (supervising radiology students). I was traveling to various hospitals around the Dayton area, working with first-year students on Tuesdays and Thursdays and second-year students on Mondays, Wednesdays, and Fridays. Clinical visits were from two to four hours per visit. My classroom hours varied by topic each quarter.

Eventually, I would branch out and teach for other departments such as allied health informatics (computers in health care) and medical terminology. At one point, I recorded a management class that was shown on local television. Students could register for my course, watch the course on TV, and then come down to the campus and take a final exam. Students could also check out a video tape of the course, watch it at their convenience, and then come to campus for a test. All were good for college credit hours.

I started freelance writing for *Advance Magazine,* located in Valley Forge, Pennsylvania. The magazine editor would usually call me with ideas on what topics of interest they would like to see. I ended up writing a monthly column regarding the management aspects of managing a radiology department. Usually, I was asked to address a specific topic, such as leasing versus purchasing radiology equipment, how to write a résumé, and how to do a job interview. This lasted for about five years, and I published 152 articles in *Advance*. I enjoyed writing, and on some occasions, I was invited to speak at local and state professional meetings such as the GDMIA (Greater Dayton Medical Imaging Association) and the OSRT (Ohio Society of Radiologic Technologists).

I was also a member of the AHRA (American Hospital Radiology Administrators) at this time and was encouraged by the hospital to attend their annual meetings. I tried to attend whenever my schedule permitted and traveled with Bev to interesting are as such as Las Vegas, Boston, and Florida. The hospital always picked up the tab, and I would file a report pointing out the insights that I had gained at the meeting.

At one point, I was contacted by the AHRA requesting that I submit an article that could be included in their upcoming textbook for radiology managers titled *Current Concepts in Radiology Management*. My chapter was titled "Facilities Project Management." My travel lectures consisted of technical or managerial aspects of radiology. Eventually, I became president of the GDMIA and resided on the OSRT board of trustees.

I was contacted by McGraw Hill from Chicago to help with editing medical textbooks. It paid well, and I could do the work from home using my laptop computer. Working under a deadline, usually a couple of weeks, I could complete the work at my leisure. Most of the books that I had assisted in editing were college textbooks dealing with medical terminology. I was assigned specific chapters of terminology, either general medical terminology or radiology imaging terms. They would email pages of text or give me access to textbook pages online, which I would then modify and return to McGraw Hill Publishers. I did this until 2012, at which time I retired from Sinclair College.

In my return to civilian life in 1975, I was able to interact more with friends and family. With my medical knowledge and expertise, I was able to assist family and friends with personal matters. For example, my previously strained relationship with the Makley family from St. Marys improved immensely once we were established back in Ohio. Bev's sister Ruth had been diagnosed with lung cancer shortly after we moved to Dayton. Ruth was living at home with her parents, John and Gretchen. She was in much pain and discomfort, spending her days and nights on the family's couch in the living room. I made calls to the local hospice center in Lima, Ohio, informing them of Ruth's situation and medical needs.

The hospice staff showed up at the Makleys' house the next day. They explained who they were and how they could assist Ruth. The provided an intravenous drip for her dehydration and put her on oxygen to help her breathe and provided other much-needed medications. By the time they left, the family had been informed that I was the one who called and requested hospice service. Gretchen and John expressed their gratitude and never forgot my good deed. These were the early days of hospice, and they did a great job of assisting patients with terminal illnesses as well as provide their families with assistance.

Ruth eventually succumbed to her illness and passed away. She was missed by family and friends and has always stayed in our memories. Since then, Bev has lost three brothers—George, Jack, and Bob Makley. Bob was the eldest and passed away on July 4, 2017, after a lengthy illness. In addition to being my brother-in-law, Bob was also a good friend and will be missed.

Throughout the years of interacting with families and friends in Ohio, I always appreciated the medical knowledge and expertise that I had gained in the navy and have, on occasion, advised friends and relatives on medical matters whenever possible. After I had retired from the navy, we took up camping, and occasionally, I would splint a suspected fracture, wrap a sprain, or simply apply first-aid ointment to a scratch. My weekend supplies always included a fully stocked first-aid kit.

1975–2012: Home Life with Family and Friends

Memorial Day cookout.   Family cookout at Grand lake St. Marys.

Soon after retiring and moving to Dayton, Bev and I decided it would be nice to have a place in St. Marys for weekend getaways. Since we already had family living in St. Marys and camping at the Rustic Haven Campgrounds, it seemed like a logical choice. My brother-in-law Bob Henning worked at the Good Year plant in St. Marys and sold campers and trailers on the side. He made me a good deal and helped set up our house trailer at the Rustic Haven Campgrounds, located on the south shore of Grand Lake St Marys.[3] Within the next year, we added a patio cover and a boat dock for our boats.

Weekend were always fun. Aggie and Marion had a trailer also, just down the road from us. My dad and Tina had a small trailer and were located in the same area as Aggie and me. Bev's parents and three brothers also routinely camped in the area. During the day, we fished, played games (horse shoes were popular), went for pontoon rides, and sat around the fire ring after dark. Of course, there was some beer drinking along the way.

One Saturday afternoon Bev and I arrived at our trailer to see Dad standing in the rain near his trailer. He apparently had been painting and had managed to get paint all over his clothes. He had just thrown his paint-covered pants into the blazing fire and then realized that his trailer keys were in his pants pocket. He ran up to our car and asked if he could borrow some tools to unlock his trailer. It only took him a minute or so to open his trailer door, where he went to dry out and put on some dry clothes.

We had to be careful when camping with Dad. Although he meant well, sometimes his good deeds could pose a problem. For example, one day he was cutting grass around his trailer and decided to do his neighbor's. While cutting her grass, Dad noticed some plastic tubing lying on the ground. He picked it up away from the trailer, not realizing that he had disconnected her oxygen. Fortunately, Dad's son-in-law Marion, who camped in the same area, heard the commotion and reconnected her oxygen. This is one of several unfortunate incidents that we witnessed during our tenure as campers at Grand Lake St. Marys.

My dad was a bit of a character, whether he was camping or at the race track, killing time at the local bar or just having fun with the family. He drove a truck, mostly interstate hauling. He loved to tell stories about his travel adventures by the campfires at night and was very popular at the campground since he was always looking

Leaving Home II

for something to do. Painting was one of his favorite pastimes. He painted anything from buildings to sheds. It was not unusual to wake up very early in the morning while it was still dark and see Dad painting his trailer or another person's camper using a lantern for light.

Weekends were fun times. One Saturday we loaded up the pontoon boat with at least twelve people and tried to cast off. However, the overload of weight made it difficult to pull away from the bank. My dad came to the rescue by jumping off the pontoon to give us a push off. Unfortunately, Dad's jump landed him a bit short, and he ended up in the water in his new white shoes.

Harry P. Hunton with grandkids.

Visiting with Relatives

In addition to staying at our trailer by the lake, we would also stay in town with relatives, especially during bad weather or around the holidays. Bev's mom and dad lived in an older two-story house on Hendricks Avenue. The house was heated by a single coal- or wood-burning stove in the living room. The heat traveled upward through a vent, providing minimal heat. Heavy blankets were needed to keep warm at night.

One of the downsides to having our bedroom directly above the downstairs vent was hearing John on the CB radio early in the morning. It was not unusual to hear him speaking to someone around 5:00 a.m. Summers were uncomfortable also. Our only means of cooling was to open a bedroom window. As the kids grew older, we got away from camping and visited the area much less.

My sister Sally lived one block away from the Makleys, and we would visit her on occasion. Linda and her cousin Sandy got along well. I remember one day when Sandy was riding her moped and offered Linda a ride. Watching from Sally's front porch, Sandy had Linda get on the back. When she was seated, Sandy took off, doing a wheelie, dumping Linda off, who landed on her butt in the road. No one was hurt, and it remains one of my funniest memories.

We had several other relatives living just ten miles east of St. Marys in Wapak, Ohio—brother Pete, his wife, Bonnie, and son, Randy. Pete's birth name was Harry P. Hunton Jr. He was named after my dad. Pete had polio as a teenager and survived with paralysis in his legs that was overcome with physical therapy. For several years, Pete operated a Sinclair gas station on the outskirts of town. These were the days when the gas station attendant would clean your windshield and fill your gas tank while you sat and watched. Pete and Mom lived in a house trailer next to the Sinclair station. On slow days, the Frederick brothers would come by, and we would play guitars and sing. Pete and I always had fun just hanging out with the guys.

Years later, Pete changed to a Marathon station in downtown Wapak, which included minor services such as oil changes and tire repair. Pete's wife, Bonnie, assisted and helped around the station. They eventually bought a house on Broadway Street in Wapak, where they raised son Randy Hunton.

Aggie and Marion lived in Wapak until they moved to Lake Okeechobee, Florida. Their children—Rick Poppe, Tami Campbell, and Tony Poppe—still reside in Wapakoneta. Sister Sally eventually moved to Florida. However, she and Aggie eventually moved back to Ohio. Sister Jackie originally lived in Norwalk, Ohio, where her husband, Lee, worked for the railroad. Years later, they moved to Lake Placid, where they still reside. Lee passed during the spring of 2018. He was well remembered at a memorial service near Norwalk, Ohio, in July 2018.

Over the years, several of our family members flew from Ohio to Florida for vacation and to visit relatives. Dad was afraid to fly and never flew. I told him that he would have to go (die) no matter where he was or what he was doing.

He replied, "Yeah, but if you are on a plane, it be time for the guy sitting next to you to go, and you have to go with him!"

Dad spent a few years in Florida and was often referred to as "dancing Harry." He was fond of dancing at bars around Lake Placid, Florida, where he worked part-time cutting grass to supplement his retirement income.

Bud Hunton

HISTORICAL EVENTS

Cuban Missile Crisis — October 1962. The U.S. Naval Hospital in Philadelphia was placed on alert. The entire staff was then restricted to area. I was assigned to work with three other chiefs to ensure that our surgical teams were ready for deployment. All equipment was inventoried and prepared for immediate deployment via Dover Air Force Base. Dover AFB in Delaware is a historic facility. During the Vietnam era, the bodies of over twenty thousand service men were transported via C-5 Galaxies to the mortuary at Dover. From here, they were escorted by uniformed service members to their final resting place. The naval hospital in Philadelphia assisted by providing active duty military escorts of similar rank. My last trip was to a small town in Georgia.

Lake Hurst, New Jersey — July 1960. A navy blimp with twenty-one crew members aboard crashed off the coast of New Jersey, one dead, taken to the naval hospital in Philadelphia for autopsy. I assisted with the X-rays in the morgue. There was a total of seventeen missing and three taken to Fort Dix, New Jersey, for treatment.

During the years 1968 to 1971, *McCard* carried drones known as ASROCs. Their purpose was to track and locate submarines that were traveling while submerged. Each drone had nuclear capabilities. On one occasion, we picked up what was referred to as a "black box" while deployed on our last Med cruise in 1968. The black box was a metal hut housing top-secret equipment that could pick up Russian communications from subs or Russian trawlers that cruised the Atlantic. We picked up the black box and three navy intelligence officers in Naples, Italy. The drones were remote-control devices that were amazingly accurate for the time they were being used. I am thankful that we did not start a nuclear war.

Leaving Home II

Four Hunton girls with cousins.

Mom and daughters Aggie, Sally, and Jackie.

Makley family at Rustic Haven.

Bud's family at Rustic Haven Campgrounds.

Typical drones that were used aboard navy destroyers to search for Russian subs.

PHOTOS

Retired from Sinclair College, 2012.

McCard, sick bay, 1971.

Bud, Bev, and girls Patty, Sue, Linda, and Debbie.

Bud at seventeen, Great Lakes, Illinois.

Leaving Home II

Family at Rustic Haven Campgrounds.

Family at home in Huber Heights, Ohio.

Bud and Bev at Navy Reunion

Bud Hunton

FMF duty, Camp Lejune, North Carolina.

Camp Lejune, North Carolina.

Aboard the USS Robert H. McCard (DD-822), 1968-1971.

The naval hospital opened in 1935 and was a health-care provider with a total of 650 beds. Considered as a state-of-the-art facility in 1935, the structure was a fifteen-story building surrounded by several wooden buildings that became recovery centers during the Vietnam era. Under the Base Realignment and Closure Act, the hospital was slated for closure and disposal. The U.S. Naval Hospital in Philadelphia was closed and all functions relocated from the complex in 1993. It was demolished on June 9, 2001, at 7:02 a.m.

U.S. Naval Hospital, Philadelphia, Pennsylvania, 1959–1963,1966–1968, 1971–1975.

Naval Terminology

At anchor	Use of a heavy device placed in water to keep the ship from drifting.
Bow	Forward part of a ship or boat.
Bulkhead	The wall.
Binnacle list	A list of crew members who are sick Excused from regular duties.
Deck	The floor.
Four-oh sailor	A sailor that is squared away. A good performer.
Gangway	A narrow passageway joining the quarter deck to the forecastle.
Hatch	A small opening on a ship (dog the hatch = close the hatch).
Head	Bathroom.
Mess deck	Where the crew goes to eat their meals.
Overhead	The ceiling.
Port	The left side of a vessel facing forward.
Quarter deck	Part of the main deck reserved for ceremonies. Station for the OOD.
Starboard	The right side of a vessel facing forward.
Sick bay	Area designated for providing medical care.
Scuttlebutt	Originally an open cask of water aboard ship. Also refers to gossip.
Stern	Aft or back part of a ship.
Swab	To use a mop ("swabbing the deck").
Squared away	Term used by all military branches to describe one whose performance is even with or above satisfactory level.
Underway	A term applied to a ship leaving port.

End Notes

1. My first name was not a problem until I was seventeen. When I joined the navy, I needed my birth certificate to prove that Bud was not just a nickname. Throughout the rest of my life, I had to frequently prove that my first name was, in fact, Bud.
2. St. Francis Hospital is a registered historic building in Cincinnati, Ohio. Opened in 1889 as St. Francis Hospital for the incurables by the Poor Sisters of St. Francis in the United States, it was initially the only hospital west of the Alleghenies with facilities to treat cancer. It operated until 1981.
3. Grand Lake St. Marys was once the world's largest artificial body of water (it was dug by 1,700 Irish and German immigrants from 1837 to 1845). It was created to supply the Miami and Erie Canal, a vital supply source connecting the Ohio River in Cincinnati and Lake Erie in Toledo.